The Paracord Bullwhip

A pictorial "how to" guide to making a 4 foot, 16 plait Bullwhip, Snakewhip and Wooden handled whip.

Copyright © 2014 Paul Carpenter

www.mtn-m.co.uk

Geared to the complete

beginner,

This book will show you

how to make a 16 plait, 4 foot

Bull and Snake whip

in my unique way.

The Paracord Bullwhip

Published by Lulu.com

ISBN number 978-1-291-92457-2

Other publications by Paul Carpenter

Travel;

Six Mountain hikes from around the World

The Moray way and the Ben Macdui Trail

Crafts;

Leather and Wood Crafts

Bows and Arrows, Homemade

Leather Armour

Leather Projects

The Leather Lace Bullwhip

Fiction;

The Rise of the Ancients

Contents

The Paracord whip

Tools and Materials..........6

Cord preparation – cord lengths - cutting and organizing..........8

Making the Core - Cord and lead shot lengths - attaching to steel pin – binding with sinew..........11

Making the Fall – Attaching Paracord needle to cord – splicing cord..........14

Braiding 1st layer – Starting braid - dropping cords - rolling whip - applying sinew and electrical tape..........15

Braiding 2nd layer – Starting braid - dropping cords – rolling whip - applying sinew – cutting end – attaching 3rd layer cords..........23

Braiding 3rd layer – Dropping cords - 16 to 14 - 14 to 12 - 12 to 10 - 10 to 8 - 8 to 6..........33

Making the 14 and 12 bight knots – components of the knots – 14b x 18p pineapple knot – 12b x 14p pineapple knot - knot foundation - attaching knots..........43

Snakewhip – braiding pattern - core – start braid for 3rd layer..........57

Wooden handles whip – braiding pattern – core - making wooden handles – tools..........63

Appendix

Making crackers and attaching them to the fall..........67

Constrictor knot..........69

Cord breaks..........70

Holding and pulling cords while braiding..........71

The Paracord whip

Whips of one sort or another have been around for centuries where the predominant material used in their construction was leather. Not so now, before the handling and use of leather left whip making in the domain of those skilled with such materials but the humble nylon Paracord now enables anyone with the will and determination to make their own robust, strong whip at a fraction of the price of a leather one.

If you are such a person, then read on and learn how to make one, or all of the whips shown on these pages.

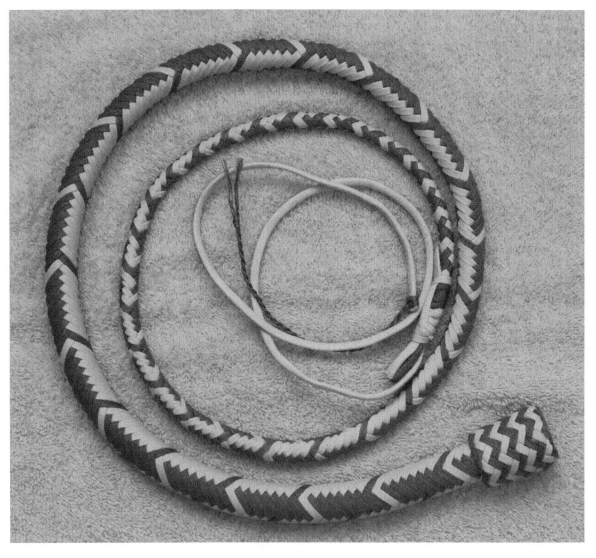

4 foot Snakewhip

4 foot Bullwhip

4 foot Wooden handled whip

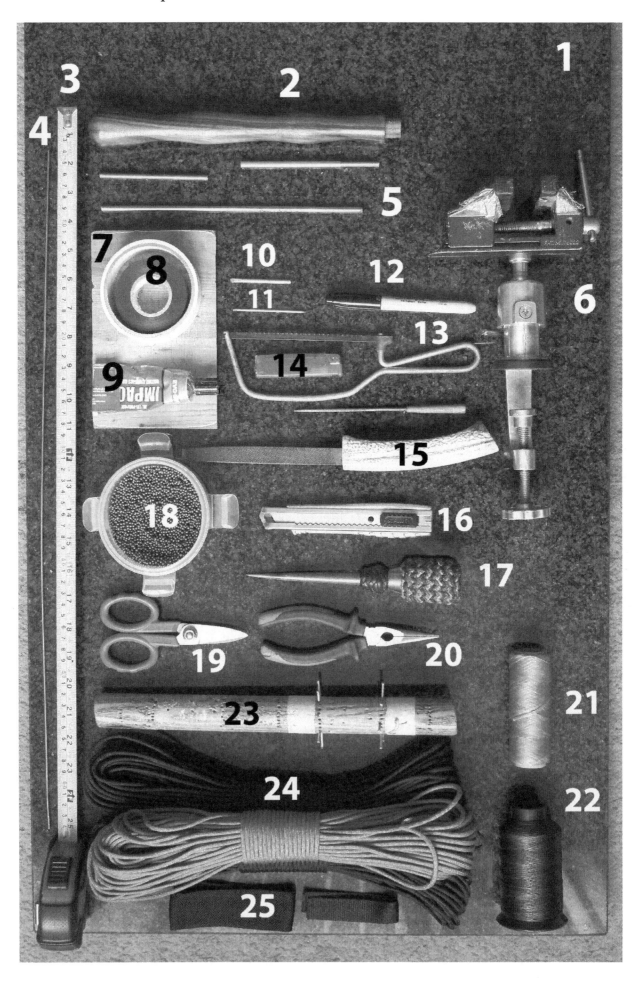

Tools and Materials

The tools listed contain certain items that I have collected in over a decade of leather and Paracord work, most however are quite common items that you may already have or could adapt from other similar tools as described below. Most, if not all of the materials are readily available from online or high street retailers.

1, Granite slab – the dimensions of mine is 21 x 34 x 1 ¾ inches. The best and cheapest place to obtain these is from places that make gravestones or even a kitchen worktop is just as good.

2, Turned wooden handle – if you have a lathe or know someone that has, then making one from a 1.5 x 1.5 x 13 inch blank of hardwood is described towards the back of this manual.

3, Tape measure, metal, 5m long.

4, Steel rod 2mm diameter, about ½ m long, to help push lead shot into Paracord.

5, Steel rod 5mm diameter, 5 inches long for wooden handle, 3 inches for Snakewhip, 9 inches for bullwhip, plus a 3 ½ inch length of 6mm copper tubing for wooden handled whip. Available from B & Q or Homebase.

6, Hobby vice with clamp to fix onto most tables with a swivel head.

7, A small piece of hardwood flooring, the samples sold in B & Q will do. Used along with the granite to roll the finished 1st, 2nd and 3rd layers.

8, Electrical tape is used on the 1st layer to aid as a bolster. Masking tape.

9, EVO-STIK impact glue 65g tube.

10, Paracord needle, you will need this for any Paracord work and the best is from Tandy leather, called a Perma Lok needle for 3/32 and 1/8th of an inch cord.

11, A Needle – I use a saddler quilting needle with a blunt end but all you need is a long needle (2 ½ inches) with a large eye to take the artificial sinew.

12, Permanent marker, fine point.

13, Junior hacksaw to cut 5mm steel rod.

14, A lighter – I have tried various lighters to help melt and fix ends of Paracord and for me, a cigarette lighter is the best offering the most control.

15, Metal file, to smooth ends of cut steel rod.

16, Hobby knife with snap off blades

17, An Awl, or long fine length of steel that tapers to a point.

18, Lead shot, 2mm diameter, advertised on eBay as diving weights.

19, Leather, cloth or any strong scissors.

20, Pliers, pointed ends

21& 22, Artificial sinew and Dacron thread, both are essential in whip construction and the best available is from here - http://www.thelongbowshop.com/. Or the Dacron is used for crackers, so any waxed twisted cotton thread should do and the sinew is available on eBay in 10m shanks (probably need about 80m)

23, Wooden dowel to make knots on along with lost head nails 25mm long. An old broomstick would do.

24, Paracord, 4mm diameter. Have used the USA and Chinese cord. Get Chinese from China on eBay and in the USA from 5star cord - http://www.fivestarcord.com/. 300ft for 4ft whip

25, Nylon webbing of 20mm (only for bullwhip) and 35mm widths used for knot foundations.

Paracord measurements for 4 foot whip

measurements for other lengths of whip - divide each length below by 4, then times by the length of whip you need. i.e 1st layer , number 3 strand, for a 6 foot whip would be;

1.2 / 4 = 0.3 x 6 = 1.8m.

Core	Lead shot	2	6	11 inches
	Paracord core	12	19	26 inches

1st layer

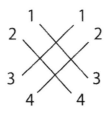

1 = 1m
2 = 1.1m
3 = 1.2m
4 = 1.5m

Sinew to 5 inches

Braid to 2 3/4 ft

2nd layer

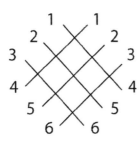

1 = 1m
2 = 1.3m
3 = 1.4m
4 = 1.6m
5 = 1.9m
6 = 2.3m

Sinew to 9 inches

3rd layer

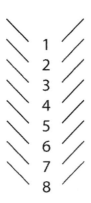

1 = 1.1m
2 = 1.5m
3 = 1.7m
4 = 1.9m
5 = 2.1m
6,7 & 8 = 2.5m

Fall & Knots (these lengths stay the same regardless of whip length)

Fall = 1.5m,
14 bight = 2 x 1.8m
12 bight = 2 x 1.5m

Lace Preparation

Many Whip makers cut the cord they need to the lengths needed, i.e. for the 1ˢᵗ layer 8 cord braid, they would cut 8 lengths of cord and then attach each lace to the whip handle by evo-stik and sinew.

I do not do this, for the 1ˢᵗ layer 8 cord braid I cut 4 lengths of lace then half them, which means there are no loose ends one end of the whip enabling a quick and easy start to the braiding of the 1ˢᵗ layer. I do this for the 1ˢᵗ and 2ⁿᵈ layers. Please note that after the 2ⁿᵈ layer, the top of the braid is cut to form a firm rounded base where the 16 cords of the 3ʳᵈ are individually fixed on, this is further explained in each layers section.

The diagram on the left displays the typical lace lengths I use to ascertain the different lengths of cord needed for a 4 foot whip for any particular braid be it the 1ˢᵗ, 2ⁿᵈ or 3ʳᵈ layer. So when I say 'Half' the lace, I mean one half maybe 1m long and the other half 1.6m as it would be for the 1 to 4 cord in the 2ⁿᵈ layer. Reason for this are to do with the gradual tapering of a whip where at various distances along the whip, cords have to be dropped.

For a 4 foot whip you will need 300 feet of Paracord and to start with I assert what colours and patterns I would like on the finished whip as shown below. Next I unravel 200ft (or all if you wish to use three colours)of it to get rid of all the twist and kinks and re-lay it on the floor to one end of the tape measure that I locked just beyond the 1m mark. Then cut, remove the 7 inner strands and lay out each cord as shown below for the 3ʳᵈ layer, or the top and therefore visible layer on the finished whip.

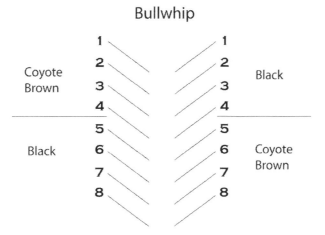

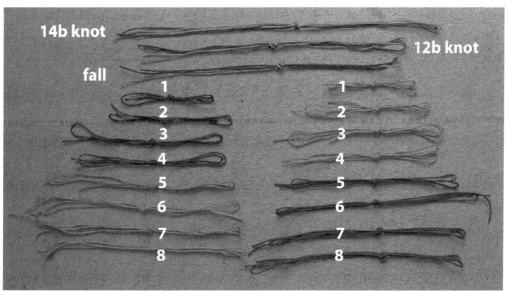

The Paracord Bullwhip

The cord for the knots and fall I place inside a plastic shopping bag and the cord for the 3rd layer I wrap in masking tape as shown below, starting with number 1 or the shortest. This ensures that when you come round to using them, they will still be in order of placing onto the finished end of the 2nd layer.

Next I cut and remove the inner strands of the cord for the 2nd layer, try to use the colours that you use for the 3rd layer, especially for the longer cords as this will, if it happens, help hide any places where there is any gaps between the braiding of the 3rd layer. For beginners this can be prone to happen where you drop from 10 to 8, and 8 to 6 cords.

Your cutting 6 cords for the 2nd layer; 2 x 1 and 4, 2 x 2 and 5, 2 x 3 and 6. Once you have cut the lengths for each cord, I find it helpful to find where the half waypoint is and then just tie it all in a knot. This ensures that when I come round to using them I will not have to find it again. Place these in the plastic bag.

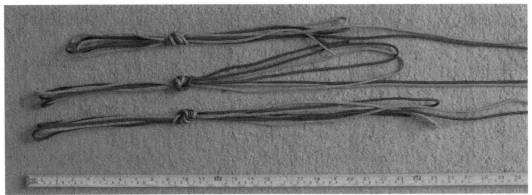

Next, you cut 4 cords and remove the inner strands for the 1st layer, 2 x 1 and 3, 2 x 2 and 4. Again, find the half waypoint, tie in a knot, and place in the plastic bag.

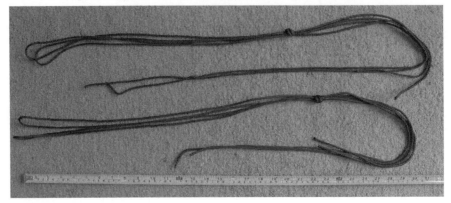

Making the Core

The measurements given on the diagram on page 8, signify the length of Paracord needed to be filled by lead shot and the length of Paracord needed. Cut these cord lengths and remove the 7 inner strands. I have found that for some reason that darker coloured Paracord is best for the core, for some reason the lead shot seems to go into it better then lighter cord.

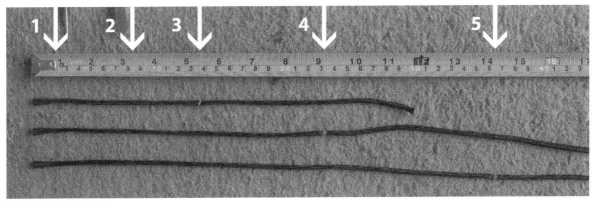

The photo above best shows each cord finished with its lead core, but first you have to burn the ends of each cord to widen them thus helping to put the lead shot in. I do this with the Awl as shown below.

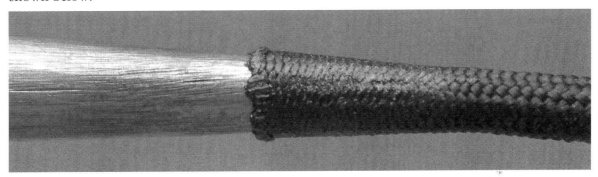

To do this push the ends as far as it will go into the awl, then run the lighter around the cord for about a second, any longer and the cord will melt and deem it useless. In addition, try not to burn below where the awl is in the cord or else again the nylon will be useless. What you are after is a wide firm funnel to which you drop the lead shot into. However, before placing the shot in you need to tie sinew at points 3, 4 and 5 as shown above.

Do this by using the saddler needle and a 1m length of sinew. Thread the sinew into the needle, then to find where to place it through the cord you need to add onto the length of shot needed the length from the ends to number 2, this includes about an inch for the funnel and 2.5 inches of empty cord, which is used to glue onto the steel pin.

Once the thread is through the cord, do a simple knot and burn ends. This is the start of you using a lighter on Paracord and you have to learn to only allow the flame to be near the cord for a split second, as it will melt very quickly and deem it useless. Not much of an issue in this instant, but when you come to dropping cord on the main layers it could wreck the whole thing if broken cord cannot be fixed as shown in the appendix.

After you have tied all three cords, you first push the 2mm rod down the cord to the tie's, this will open up the cord. Next start putting the lead shot in. I start by dropping a few into the funnel while twisting the end gently, then use the 2mm steel rod to push them down to the tie's.

Once you have filled all 3 cords with the lead shot to number 2 in the photo opposite, then cut at number 1 to get rid of the funnel part, place them all on a flat surface with the parts between 1 and 2 hanging over the edge and apply evo-stik to the full 2.5 inches length.

Next get the 9 inch steel pin and make firm in the vice and mark on it with the marker pen 2 inches from one end – apply evo-stik to this as well.

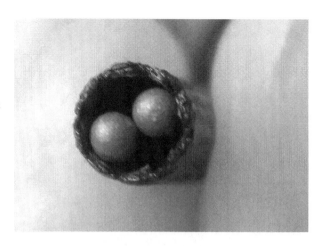

Once the glue has dried, apply each cord to the steel pin, first by pressing the start of the lead shot against the pins end and then down the pin to the marker. Do this evenly around the pin.

Next starting about 2 inches back from the cord; bind the sinew onto the steel pin towards the cord as shown on the next page. Once you reach the end of the steel pin and the start of the lead shot, bind around tight once more and then run the sinew, as shown above, loosely down to the end of the first cord of lead, then run loosely back up to the start of the pin, tie off and burn end of sinew to secure. The tight binding of the sinew over the pin is to tighten the hold of it onto the pin, whereas the loose binding is just to keep these three cords together making the braiding of the 1st layer easier.

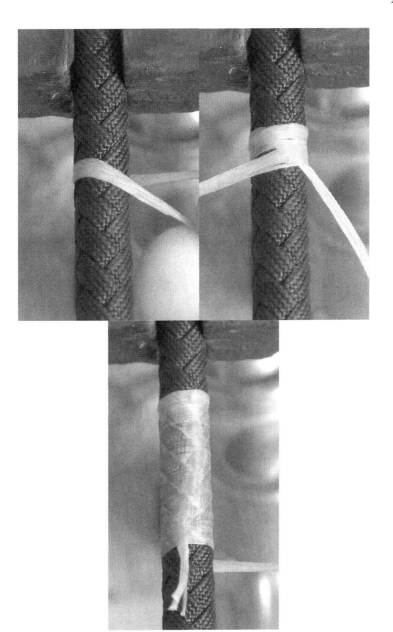

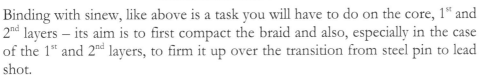

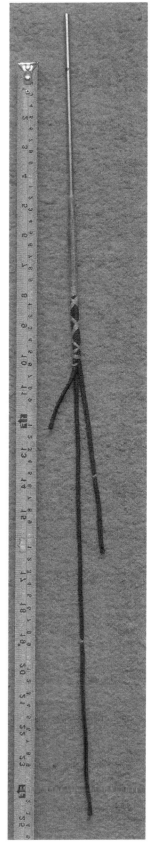

Binding with sinew, like above is a task you will have to do on the core, 1st and 2nd layers – its aim is to first compact the braid and also, especially in the case of the 1st and 2nd layers, to firm it up over the transition from steel pin to lead shot.

Looking from left to right, wrap the bottom strand over the top strand a couple of turns before letting loose of the top one, then bind the sinew around for the desired length needed down the braiding keeping the sinew as tight as possible.

The core is the essence of a whip, how it is constructed will determine the look of the finished whip. The whips I make not only have a slight taper in the handle (created by gluing the 2 inches onto the end of the steel pin) but also more importantly, have a gradual taper throughout the whip. This is created by shortening the three core cords below where their lead shot stops to certain ratio's that are the same for any length of whip.

As can be seen opposite, the shorter cord is cut half way between the seconds length bf lead shot. The second cord is cut half way between the end of its lead shot and the start of the third longest cord. The longest cord is cut to a distance equal to the difference between where it's lead and that of the second longest lead stops.

Making the Fall

In order to make the fall, you have to thread the cord onto the Paracord needle, the best way of which I have found is shown below. It is best to make the fall now as your need it to end the 3rd layer.

Going from left to right, burn one of the cord you cut for the fall. Do not keep the lighter stationary in one position but run it over the end for a second, then between thumb and finger press the cord end. Next cut the cord at an angle and burn again the same way, but this time twists the end of the cord between thumb and finger to create a point. It is ready to screw into the needle. Test it before proceeding to see that it will not come off. The reason for doing the first burn is that if you had not, the end would fray and you would not get as sharp a point as displayed above.

Find the half waypoint of the cord (top photo) and use the awl to puncture a hole into it (middle bottom photo). Place the needle into this hole and push down the length of the cord (bottom right photo). To do this hold the end of the needle while pushing the outer cord over front of it, then release the end while holding the front allowing the bunched up cord to go backwards. In essence, you are making what is called a splice, the object of which is to make a loop (bottom left photo) try as much as you can to ensure that there is no twist in this loop, it's not a disaster if there is, it will just look better without them.

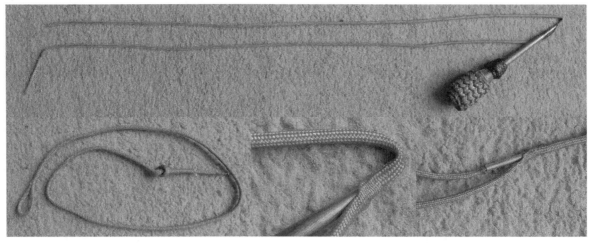

Braiding 1ˢᵗ layer

The photo on the right illustrated the core with numbers that indicate the points at which you will need to drop cords. Unlike on the 3ʳᵈ layer where the cords are dropped in two's and tied in place with sinew, I only drop one cord at a time on the 1ˢᵗ and 2ⁿᵈ layers and do not tie them, just burn and glue them onto the braid.

This will be further explained in the proceeding pages, for now the photo merely shows you where along the core you will need to drop 4 cords, leaving 4 to extend beyond the core and make a tapered end to a length of 2 ¾ to 3 foot as written on the measurement diagram on page 8.

You will also notice on the photo that I have placed a black mark on the top of the steel pin from where the tape is extended. Despite the fact that I am using a 9-inch steel pin, I have planned for the handle to be 7 inches long. The reason for the 2 inches, of what will be essentially waste and later cut away is that at the point where you start the braiding, it can and probably will be lumpy i.e. not perfectly round, which would effect the effectiveness of the foundation and make the knot look terrible. The white line is merely an indication of the end of the 1ˢᵗ layer.

To avoid this I start the braiding above that mark, meaning that the lumps will be cut out later leaving a perfectly round end where the cord will be firmly fixed by glue and sinew.

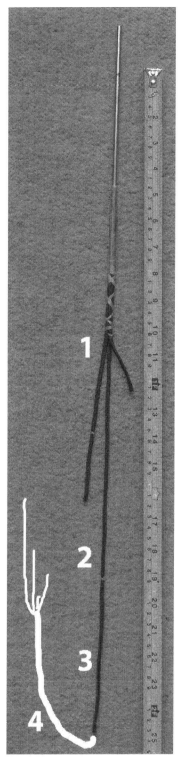

Another reason for the extended steel pin is to allow you extra length of a solid base in which to aid braiding tightly as it means (as shown below) that you can extend the pin further out from the vice and braid further along the handle before moving it.

One further point, when I start illustrating braiding, I will be mentioning a lot of Unders and Overs. This merely indicates the action you should take with the cord to be braided i.e. If I say "thread under 2 over 2" it means you thread the cord under 2 cords and then over two cords. In all cases, the cord which will be braided is the upper most one of both left and right sides.

If at any point you need to leave the braiding, such as the doorbell rings etc, try to drape the ends over the vice to keep the left and right separate. When you return, first pull and tighten all cords before proceeding to ensure they keep that even tightness.

Start the braid by removing the 1st layer cords from your plastic bag and lay them in their pairs on a chair or something similar, then going from the left to right photo, top to bottom;

1, Lay the midpoints of the two shorter cords as thus leaving the longer ends nearest to you.

2 Lay the remaining two cords as thus laying the longer ends nearest to you. Take number 1 and thread back under 2 and over two.

3, Take number 2 and again thread back under 2 and over 2

4,5, 6, 7 Following the same Under 2 and Over 2 sequence as above, braid each of the number cords, 3, 4, 5, 6.

8, Continue with the sequence Under 2 Over for a couple more turns2 ensuring you braid the upper most cord. Once you have reached this length push the awl through the middle of the braid.

9, take the braid off of the awl and place onto the steel pin as shown. Pulling the upper right cord first, tighten all the cords onto the pin

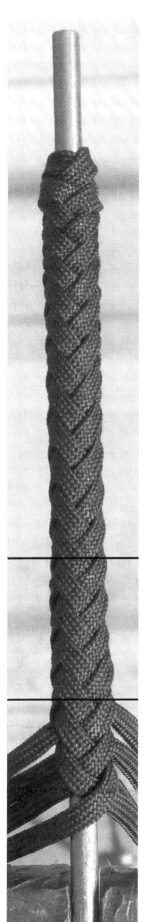

Before braiding any further, apply Evo-stik to the steel pin from the end of the braiding to the start of the lead shot. This is not to stick the cord to the steel pin, but allow some friction between the cord and the smooth surface of the steel pin as sometimes; even after applying sinew the braid along the handle will move on a finished whip over time.

After the glue has dried, continue braiding down the length of the steel pin in the Under 2 Over 2 sequence using the "holding and Pulling method" I have demonstrated in the appendix, as from now on you have to ensure the braid is tight.

Despite keeping the cords as tight as you can while braiding, there is a length of braid that will not be very tight, as marked on the left photo between the black lines. This is normal, just ensure when you move the braiding from the front of the vice to the back that you do not clamp over this area, as shown on the right.

For all round braiding with or without a core within it, when you braid a cord you first have to move it around the back and then make the under and over movements on its opposing set of cord, as demonstrated below during a under 2, over 2, under 2, over 2 braiding sequence.

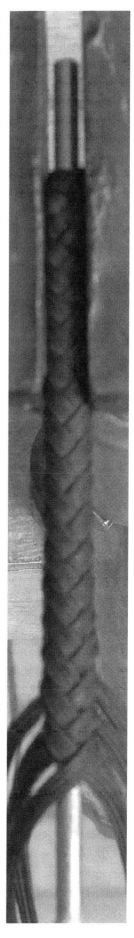

Continue braiding down until you get to the point where you need to drop the first cord. This will be at the end of the shortest length of lead shot where the sinew you wrapped ends.

The cord you will drop is the shortest on the right side, sometimes it is not the cord that matches up exactly with the end of the lead shot, don't worry the little bit it may go beyond is no problem.

The cord in question is marked X above and is not as much dropped but joined into the cords of the core;

From left to right - 1, indicates the cord to be dropped, 2, braid the top left side cord as usual, 3, Braid the top right side cord as usual but allowing X to drape down into the core cords.

Carrying on with the bottom photo, left to right – 4, Braid the top left cord under 2 and then Over 1. 5, Braid the top right cord under 2 and still over 2 (the sequence of braiding from right to left still stays the same as there is still the same amount of cords on the left side) 6, Braid the top left cord under 2 and over 1.

Carry on this braid sequence of on the left under 2 and over 1 and the right under 2, over 2 until you near the next dropping point.

After you have braided this sequence for about 2 inches, you need to pull the cord that was X within the core cords. Once that is done, you can cut it off at a point just above where the second drop occurs, or number 2 in the diagram on page 15.

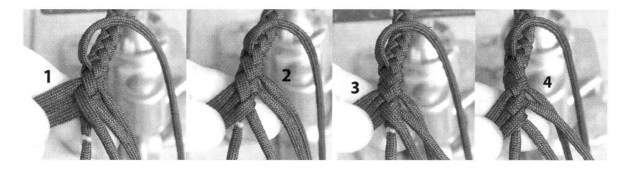

Upon reaching g the second drop from 7 to 6 cords (at 18 inches along the whip), it is the top left cord that is just left hanging. Following the photo above;

Braid **Number 1,** under 2 and over 1. **Number 2,** under 2 and over 1. **Number 3,** under 2 and over 1. **Number 4,** under 2 and over 1. Following on with this braiding sequence until the next drop.

Upon reaching the third drop from 6 to 5 cords (at roughly 22 inches) it is the top right that is to be dropped. Following the photo above;

Braid **Number 1,** under 2 and over 1. **Number 2,** under 1 and over 1. **Number 3,** under 2 and over 1. **Number 4,** under 1 and over 1. Following on with this braiding sequence until the next drop.

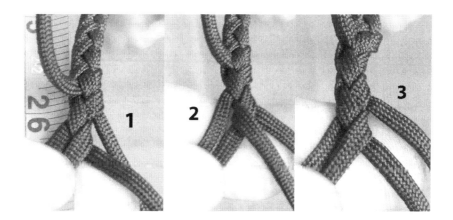

Upon reaching the dropping of the left cord from 5 to 4 cords at 26 inches. Start with the top left cord, braid as following from left to right;

Braid **Number 1** under 1 and over 1. **Number 2** under 1 and over 1. **Number 3** under 1 and over 1.

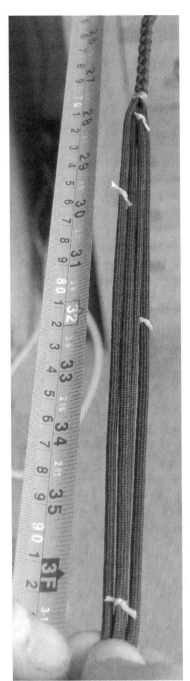

Carry on with the sequence for another 3 inches, then apply a constrictor knot at roughly 28 inches, as shown in the photo on the left (see appendix on how to tie the constrictor knot)

Once you tie off the end of the braiding, this leaves you with four loose cords. These will be cut at different lengths as marked opposite with the sinew ties.

The first and shortest is cut near to where you applied the constrictor knot, the fifth is cut at 3feet with the second and third cut at equal distances between the first and fourth.

This ratio of the lengths for the second and third cord i.e a third of the distance between each cord will be the same for any length of whip.

Saying that, when it comes to the longest cord, I tend to use the length of 3 foot only as an aid in finding the correct cutting lengths of the others and tend to leave it a half foot longer, cutting it to size later during the braiding of the 2nd layer. The reason for this is that while braiding the 2nd layer over it, it does tend to shorten as its pull upwards, pulling it as you braid helps but leave some extra for safety.

To help stop having all these cords flapping around, I use the same procedure that I used for the fall to place the longest cord into the third longest as illustrated below.

This will involve placing the Paracord needle onto the end of the longest cord and then using the awl to make a hole into the third longest at about 3 inches from the end of the braiding. You do it this close to the braiding in order to make a loop for the second longest cord to go into and essentially be trapped in place.

Once that is finished, the whip will look similar to the bottom right photo.

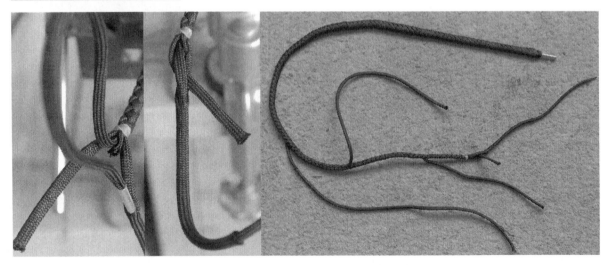

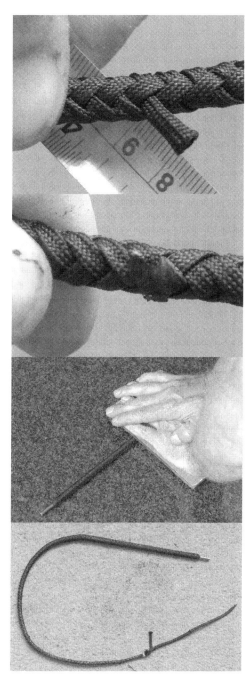

Next, pull the three dropped cords to make sure they are tight and cut as shown on the left.

Take care burning the ends of these with a lighter, remember just run it over the end for a second and then with your thumb push the cord up and round to roughly a 45 degree angle, thus following the angle of braid.

Next comes the rolling. This is another of those important acts in the making of whips, how well or badly you do it depends on the smooth or rough look of the whip.

I find it best to place the granite slab (if you have one) on the floor so that I can get my whole weight behind the act of rolling. I use a piece of wooden flooring instead of a metal bar (as other might) as it is wide enough for me to place both hands directly over the whip.

Starting at the handle end and roll back and forwards about 2 or 3 times, do this down the length of the whip until you reach the point where the constrictor knot is. It is at the very narrow end where problems seem to occur, such as the dropped cords coming away from the whip or bends where they were dropped. Just burn them back on and as for the bend. Keep rolling up and down the whip for at least 3 times, or more if you fell it needs it.

After the rolling it's time to place the electrical tape on, which acts like a bolster, plus like the sinew, will firm the whip up slightly. I place two layers of it over a 4 foot whip, for a 5 foot and above, 3 layers is better finished again at equal distances between the start of the lead shot and the second dropped cord.

Start the first tape 1 inch before the end of the steel pin and wrap tightly to 14 inches. Start the second layer an inch behind the first and wrap to the second dropped cord, or 19 inches as marked on the photo to the right.

The far right image shows the taped whip with two black markings, these indicate the end of the steel pin and to where I wrap the sinew. The method I use to apply the sinew was shown earlier and I start wrapping it about 2 inches back from the tape, ensuring I wrap it very tightly a few inches either side of the steel and lead shot area.

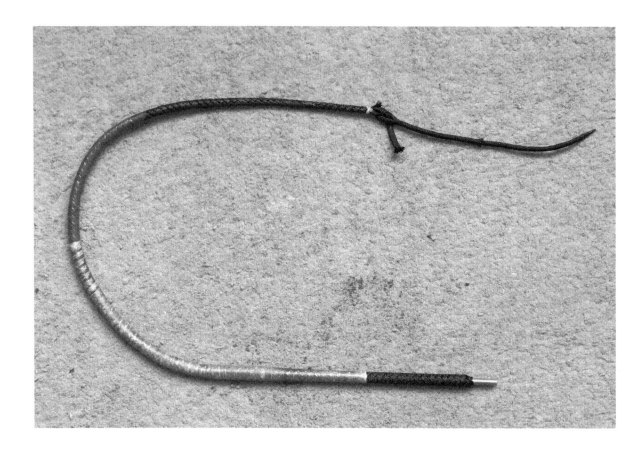

Above is the finished 1st layer, showing the extent of the tape and the sinew wrapping. It goes without saying that you have probably gathered by now that anything that goes into making a whip is applied with force to make it tight. When applying the sinew, if you do not see the pattern of the braid coming through it or the Paracord bulge as you apply it, then you're not doing it tight enough. But no worries if you haven't, my first whip would have been better served as a colander than a whip it had that many gaps in it.

Braiding 2nd Layer

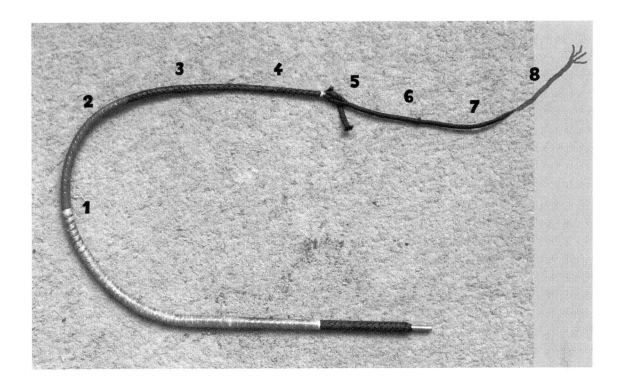

The photo above illustrates the dropping of the 8 cords in the 2nd layer. Their distances are again a ratio that can be used for any length of whip.

The first 4 cords need to be dropped before the end of the braiding which are (as much that is possible) spaced out between just beyond the sinew wrapping or where the diameter of the whip starts to narrow and about 2 inches above where the braiding of the 1st layer stops.

The fifth cord is dropped half way before the shorter 1st layer cord finishes. The sixth 1.5 inches before the next 1st layer cord finishes, the seventh 2 inches before the last 1st layer cord finishes. The eight cord, after cutting the 1st layers longest cord to 35 inches was dropped on this whip at 35 inches where upon I continued braiding for a further 2 inches before applying the constrictor tie.

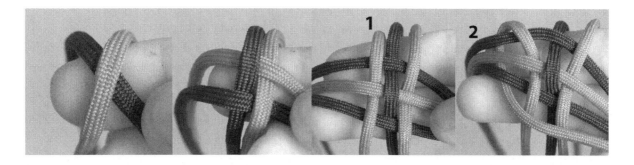

As with the 1st layer, start by laying out the cords of the 2nd layer, starting with the shortest, lay on your fingers as shown above laying the shorter length of each cord away from you.

Next start the braiding with top right cord, **Number 1**, going under 3 and over 3, then the top left cord, **Number 2** going under 3 and over 3.

Braid the top right cord, **Number 3**, going under 3 and over 3. **Number 4** going under 3 and over 3. **Number 5** (the lighter cord) going under 3 and over 3. Next **Number 6** going under 3 and over 3.

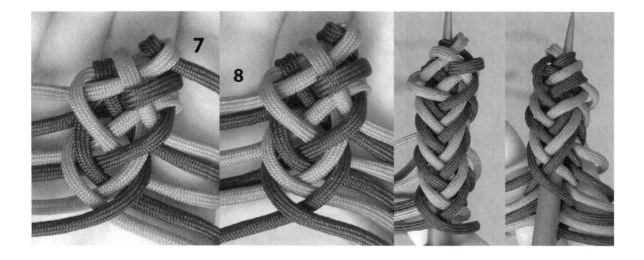

Braid the top right cord **Number 7** going under 3 and over 3.**Number 8** going under 3 and over 3. Carry on braiding in this under 3 and over 3 sequence for a couple more turns, then insert the awl into the braid making sure you check the front and back to ensure the awl is all the way through the middle of the braid.

Remove the braiding from the awl carefully and place onto the end of the handle. Ensure it rest above the cords of the 1st layer, then tighten all cords. Next, proceed to tightly braid in the under 3 over 3 sequence down the length of the handle until you get next to the vice. Then remove from the vice and place the top of the handle into it. Carry on braiding the under 3 and over 3 sequence.

There is no need to tie in any of the cords dropped on this or the 1st layer as they are held in place enough by the braiding they came from, plus because they were further secured by melting them in place.

Dropping cord, this way on these layers also helps to prevent too much bulking and lumps along the whip.

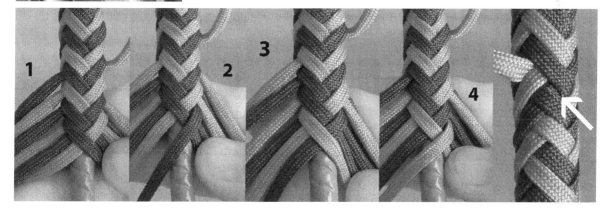

At the 1st drop, you will be going from 12 to 11 cords by dropping the upper right hand cord. Then as illustrated above;

Braid the top left cord, **Number 1**, under 3 and over 2. **Number 2,** under 3 and over 3. **Number 3,** under 3 and over 2. **Number 4,** under 3 and over 2. Carry on with this sequence until the next drop. The last photo illustrates the gap that you will leave at this drop. Do not worry about it, it will be filled after the dropped cord is cut and melted into place as shown in the photo above

At the 2nd drop, you will be going from 11 to 10 cords by dropping the upper left hand cord. Then as illustrated above;

Braid the top left cord, **Number 1,** under 3 and over 2. **Number 2,** under 3 and over 2. **Number 3,** under 3 and over 2. **Number 4,** under 3 and over 2. Carry on with this sequence until the next drop.

At the 3nd drop, you will be going from 10 to 9 cords by dropping the upper right hand cord. Then as illustrated above;

Braid the top right cord, **Number 1,** under 3 and over 2. **Number 2,** under 2 and over 2. **Number 3,** under 3 and over 2. **Number 4,** under 2 and over 2. Carry on with this sequence until the next drop.

At the 4th drop, you will be going from 9 to 8 cords by dropping the upper left hand cord. Then as illustrated above;

Braid the top left cord, **Number 1,** under 2 and over 2. **Number 2,** under 2 and over 2. **Number 3,** under 2 and over 2. **Number 4,** under 2 and over 2. Carry on with this sequence until the next drop.

At the 5th drop, you will be going from 8 to 7 cords by dropping the upper right hand cord. Then as illustrated above; Note the distance to the end of the cord under the braiding.

Braid the top right cord, **Number 1,** under 2 and over 2. **Number 2,** under 2 and over 1. **Number 3,** under 2 and over 2. **Number 4,** under 2 and over 1. Carry on with this sequence until the next drop.

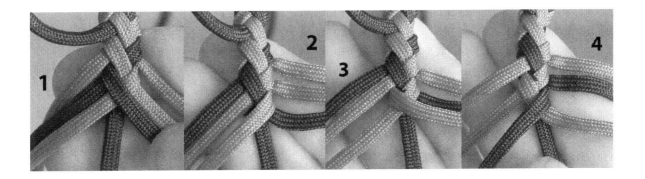

At the 6th drop, you will be going from 7 to 6 cords by dropping the upper left hand cord. Then as illustrated above;

Braid the top left cord, **Number 1,** under 2 and over 1. **Number 2,** under 2 and over 1. **Number 3,** under 2 and over 1. **Number 4,** under 2 and over 1. Carry on with this sequence until the next drop.

At the 7th drop, you will be going from 6 to 5 cords by dropping the upper right hand cord. Then as illustrated above; Note the distance to the end of the cord under the braiding.

Braid the top left cord, **Number 1,** under 2 and over 1. **Number 2,** under 1 and over 1. **Number 3,** under 2 and over 1. **Number 4,** under 1 and over 1. Carry on with this sequence until the next drop.

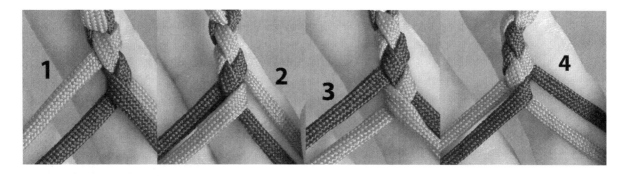

At the 8th drop, you will be going from 5 to 4 cords by dropping the upper left hand cord. Then as illustrated above;

Braid the top left cord, number **1**, under 1 and over 1. Braid number **2**, under 1 and over 1. Braid number **3**, under 1 and over 1. Braid number **4**, under 1 and over 2.

Carry on with this sequence until you get to 39 inches as illustrate to the left and tie a constrictor knot.

The way you cut the last four cords differs slightly at the end of the 2nd layer to that of the 1st layer. The first cord is still cut next to the constrictor knot, and the second is cut 6 inches from the knot, but the third and fourth cord are not cut, merely one is put inside the other with the Paracord needle making the entry as before, half way along the second cord. As shown before on page 20 as per the first layer. The third and fourth cords will be about 5 or more feet long, you need them that long do not cut them down.

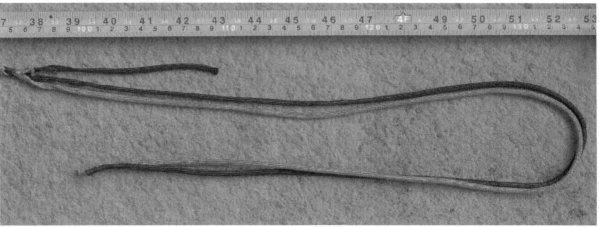

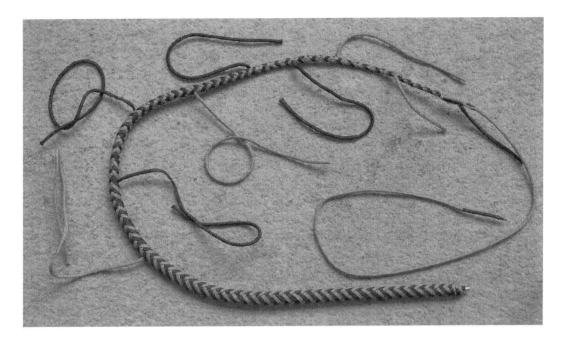

The photo above illustrates the 2nd layer braided on with all the dropped cords. Proceed to cut these and melt into place.

Next job is to wrap the sinew from the beginning of the handle to 9 inches beyond it down the whip as shown in the left photo. There is no need for electrical tape or bolster on this layer; it's only needed on the 1st layer.

Next make a mark 2 inches from the end of the steel pin, apply sinew and electrical tape (to hold the sinew in place as you cut it) about an inch either side of the mark as shown in the last two photos.

Cut all the Paracord away from the steel pin, by first using the hobby knife to score just above the marker all the way around down to the steel rod. Then after securing the whip into the vice start a cut from the cut you have just done all the way to the end of the braiding. Once all the cord is off, use the lighter to burn the exposed ends of the cord and around the edge of the cut.

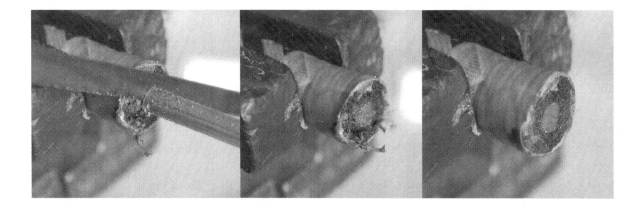

Using a junior hacksaw, cut away the remainder of the steel rod, file down if needed and burn the end once again with the lighter if needed.

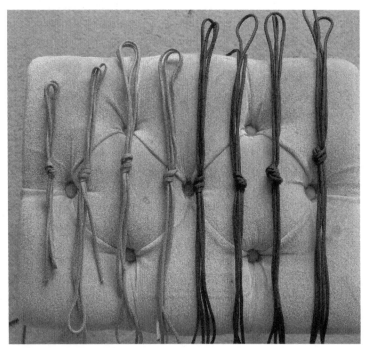

The end of the whip should look nice and even, with all uneven lumps cut away and the burning of the end has also helped secure it all in place.

Position the whip in the vice ready for you to glue on the cords of the 3rd layer, plus lay one set of the 3rd layer cords out in order of them going on. I prefer to apply the shortest first working up to the longest, plus I prefer doing this job late in the day as leaving the glue to set as long as possible before pulling on it will allow the glue to set stronger.

I start gluing the first set of the 3rd layer on from right to left, laying each at roughly a 45 degree angle, the same angle the cord goes when braided.

First, apply glue to the top of the whip to a depth of 1 inch and apply the same amount to the end of each cord. Leave them to dry for 5 or so minutes and then start attaching them.

Starting with the shortest cord lay them on as illustrated in the photo on the left leaving a very slight gap between each to ensure they evenly cover the circumference of the whip.

Once they are on cut a piece of sinew about 1m long, drape over the cords and make a constrictor knot. Tighten this on about half an inch down from the top and wind each end round the constrictor knot above and below it ensuring that you pull each end as tight as you can as you go. Tie off with a double over hand knot and burn the ends. The depth you want to wrap in sinew is 1 inch. Lastly burn the end of the whip and press down with your thumb, this help to melt and secure the sinew better as well as flattening the ends of the cord.

Next apply glue onto the end of the whip over the sinew and the ends of the other set of cords just as before.

Apply the shortest cord as before, but this time you apply them from left to right.

Before starting, ensure that you are applying the shortest of this second set above the shortest cord of the first set as shown by the arrow above right.

When applying these cords, ensure that they lay between the cords of the first set where the sinew stops, this will help the braiding of the 3rd layer.

As you lay each of these cords, leave a wider gap between each to accommodate the wider diameter. Then wrap in sinew again, tie off and burn the end.

This is the 2nd layer finished.

The Paracord Bullwhip

Braiding 3rd layer

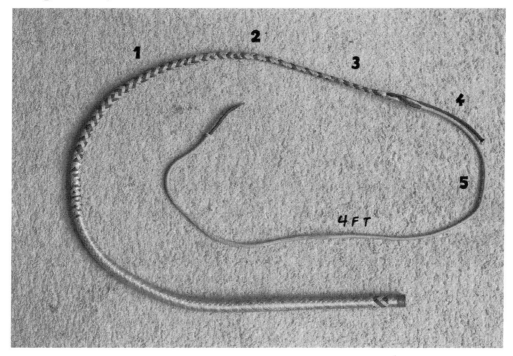

The photo above illustrates where pairs of cords are dropped in the 3rd layer. Their distances are again a ratio/measurement that can be used for any length of whip.

As a rule, I first mark where I will drop the pair before the braiding ends. So, starting with number 3, I drop these cords about 2 inches above the end of the braiding (this distance will be the same for any length whip) then measure 8 inches up to number 2 and another 8 inches to number 1(this 8 inch can be divided by 4 and times by a whip length).

I mark these points with the permanent pen; they are not necessarily, where I will drop. Their purpose is to help me see the area they should be dropped. The where and when of dropping cords in this layer depends on the tapering of the whip and the amount of bunching up of the cords this creates. You cannot afford any gaps between cords in this layer.

The next two pair are dropped first at number 4, this is half way along the short cord as seen above. Then number 5 is dropped between 5 to 6 inches before the full 4 foot length is reached.

You will not be cutting the long double ply length of cord, this runs the entire length of the whip and will only be cut once the fall in tied on.

So far, the braiding sequences have been fairly simple and straight forward, but for a bullwhip, it is customary to braid different pattern along the handle, to that braided along the whip. You may have seen various bullwhips with fancy patterns braided along the handle only to see a more normal pattern after the 12 bight knot, or transition knot (whose job is to hide this changing of pattern as well as signify the end of the handle and start of the whip – this is covered more in the knot chapter)

In order to do these fancy patterns you would need to have all the left cords of one colour and those of the right another. It is not possible to do these fancy braids with this whip due to the way the 3rd layers cords colours are attached, but you will create a different pattern nonetheless along the handle to that along the whip by a simply change of Overs and Unders.

A sequence of Under 2, over 2, under 2, over 2 will be used for each cord along the handle (remember the amount of Unders and Overs, in this case 8, equals the amount of cords on one side of the braiding, not the whole amount of cords being used, which is 16). Once the transition point is reached, the braid will revert to Under 4, Over 4.

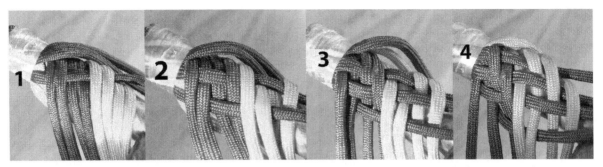

Place the whip in the vice, drape the bottom set of cords towards the left and the top set towards the right as shown above, the cords at the very front should be the two shortest cord of each set. Plus, using your permanent marker, mark the end of the handle at 7 inches and another mark 20mm above that, this will aid you in knowing when to change from the handle braid to the whip braid.

When braiding this sequence, which is just getting each cord in its right place for the handle braid, I will be writing the sequence as it needs to be braidied from the bottom to top, or as seen in each photo above, from right to left. I do this as the amount of over or unders near the sinew may differ on your whip to this one.

Number 1, over 2, under 2, over 2, under 2. **Number 2,** under 1, over 2, under 2, over 2, under 1. **Number 3,** under 2, over 2, under 2. **Number 4,** over 1, under 2, over 2, under 1.

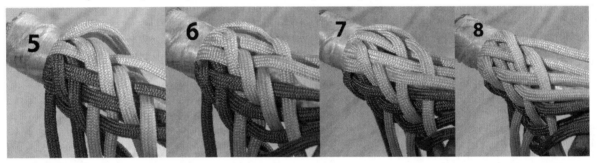

Number 5, over 2, under 2. **Number 6,** under 1, over 2, under 1. **Number 7,** under 2, over 2. **Number 8,** over 1, under 1.

The start of the braid should look like the photo top left where you can see the start of the under 2 and over 2 pattern created by the cords. If it is not, then just try again, it personally took me loads of whips to get this bit.

From now on the main braiding is starting;

Take the top left hand cord, **Number 1**, go under the handle then up going under 2, over 2, under 2, over 2 on its opposing set of cords on the right. Do the same movement for the top right hand cord, **Number 2**.

Take the top left hand cord, **Number 3**, go under the handle then up going under 2, over 2, under 2, over 2 on its opposing set of cords on the right. Do the same movement for the top right hand cord, **Number 4**.

Carry on with this sequence until you reach the pair of shortest cords, as shown on the left.

When I braid the 3rd layer I prefer to braid in sets of 8, meaning 8 pairs of cord at a time ending with the shortest cords each time. My purpose for this is to push up the braiding about 2 to 4mm, then tighten each cord one side at a time. This is to ensure that no gaps appear between the cords where the whip is widest and to keep the braid tight.

Keeping note of the amount of sets you braid also helps aid in knowing where to drop cords.

For this 4 foot whip, it took 7 sets of push and tight, plus 2 further sets of just tighten to reach the first drop (these are counted after the transition knot where the braiding patterns changes). A further 5 sets to the second drop and 4 to the next.

After you have pushed and tightened all the cords, check all the way around the braiding and check that the braiding looks correct 30mm from the top, the top knot will hide any gaps above that. Do this check after braiding each set until at least after the second drop.

Carry on with the 4-sequence braiding along the handle until you come level with the mark you made at 7 inches, as shown on the left.

This is where you change the braiding pattern to under 4 and over 4 as shown on the next page.

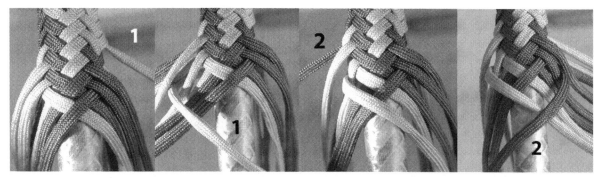

Start with the top right cord **Number 1,** under 4, over 4. Top left cord, **Number 2,** under 4, over 4.

Top right cord, **Number 3**, under 4, over 4.

Continue with this sequence of braid until you come to the shortest cord, push up and tighten. The change from the handle braid to this whip braid should look as shown on the top right photo going from left to right; front view, left side view, back view.

Continue braiding the sequence of under 4 and over 4 in sets down to where you make the first drop. Ensure you pull each cord evenly to create the straight braid as shown on the left, use the sets to alter or adjust this if necessarily.

As you near the first dropping of cords, they will all bunch up slightly. The photo below shows, on the left the cords not bunched, and on the right, bunched. The difference in the photo does not look much, but when you come to braiding, you will feel them gather, and you may experience difficulty performing the correct

under and over movement. Once they start bunching, I braid another set after that before I drop the cords.

To drop a pair of cords, you need them to be the bottom pair as indicated above left. First place the whip near to the vice, tighten all cords including those you drop and drape the others over the vice to keep them out of the way. Take hold of the pair of cords to be dropped and turn them once around the whip then tie off with a constrictor knot.

Pull the cords to be cut again and retighten the constrictor knot, then cut the sinew ends off near to the cord and burn their ends pushing them down to fix below the knot. Take care when burning the sinew ends as they are near to the draped cords above and you would only need to brush them with heat to weaken them and perhaps cause a break.

Cut the right cord about an inch below the constrictor knot and the left cord 2 inches. Burn their ends and push onto the whip smoothing them down to ensure they create a even hold onto the whip.

This is the braid from 16 to 14 cords; Number 1, under 4, over 3. **Number 2**, under 4, over 3. **Number 3**, under 4, over 3.

Braid of 16 to 14 continued. **Number 3,** under 4, over 3. **Number 4,** under 4, over 3.

The photo with the arrow illustrates where the cords dropped is under the cords you have just braided below it. As you braid on downwards keep an eye on both sides of the braiding just below this point as the dropped cords could potentially cause a gap either side if the cords were not bunched up enough before you dropped them, as marked by the end of the awl on the end photos. If you do encounter gaps here, just push the cords up to try to close them. Carry on with this sequence until the next drop.

This is the braid from 14 to 12 cords. Tie off and secure the dropped cords as before. Before starting to braid beware that due to the Unders and Overs in this move, the first two cords you braid will try to roll over the cords you have just dropped as shown in the first photo above. See the next page about more on this.

Starting top left, **Number 1,** under 3, over 3. **Number 2,** under 3, over 3.

Number 3, under 3, over 3. **Number 4,** under 3, over 3.

Carry on with this sequence until the next drop.

The first photo above displays how the braided cords will try to roll over and hide the dropped cords beneath them. You need these to be visible as shown in the third photo, I find it helpful to push that point up towards me as I tighten the cords. Also, check either side at this point to check that there are no gaps.

This is the braid from 12 to 10 cords showing the distance from the end of the braiding of the 2nd layer. Tie off and secure the dropped cords as before.

Number 1, under 3, over 2. **Number 2,** under 3, over 2.

Number 3, under 3, over 2. **Number 4,** under 3, over 2. Check for gaps.

Carry on with this sequence until the next drop. Upon nearing the end of the braiding of the 2nd layer, tighten the cords even more as this is a weak point.

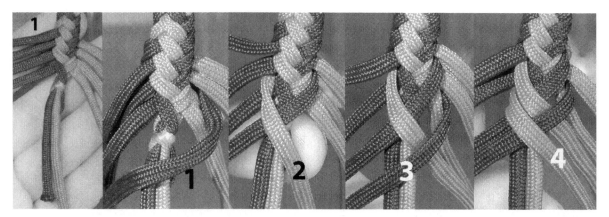

This is the braid from 10 to 8 cords. The first photo above displays the distance from the end of the 2nd layers cord. Tie off and secure the dropped cords as before. This is another braid that could see the braiding roll over the dropped cords.

Starting top left, **Number 1,** under 2, over 2. **Number 2,** under 2, over 2. **Number 3,** under 2, over 2. **Number 4,** under 2, over 2.

Check for gaps and carry on with this sequence until the next drop. Remember to pull the inner doubled cord now and again to stop it being drawn up into the braid.

This is the braid from 8 to 6. The first photo displays at what distance along the whip I dropped these cords.

Starting top left, **Number 1** under 2, over 1. **Number 2,** under 2, over 1.

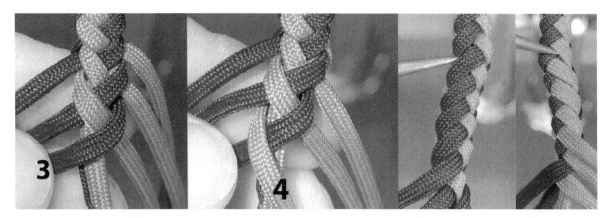

Number 3, under 2, over 1. **Number 4,** under 2, over 1.

Ensure you check the gap on this drop as it is the one drop most likely to have wide ugly ones'. Again if they appear, push the cords up to help cover them.. A little gap as shown in the last photo, is acceptable as it will be hidden after rolling the whip.

After I have dropped my last pair of cords, I place the tape measure on the floor, using it to check just how long the whip is. Once you reach 4 foot (or beyond) tighten the six remaining cord and turn the whip over in the vice. Re tighten the cords and thread the fall through them as shown in the last four photos above bringing it to rest by the vice. Lastly tighten its loop over the whip.

Drape the fall over the remaining cords as shown above left. Start with the upper most cord, **Number 1,** loop it over the fall, under the whip and thread it back through the loop you have just made. Pull it tight down and away from you, then lay along the fall towards you. Repeat the same procedure with **Number 2**, **Number 3**, (photo below) **Number 4, Number 5** and finally **Number 6**. Ensure you tie all of them from right to left.

If your upper most cord happens to be on the left, then loop them all over from left to right. It's not really important which you use.

Keeping **Number 6** separate from the others, proceed to tighten each of the 6 cords. Next you need to cut the excess of the core. Make sure it is not the fall before proceeding.

To cover the end of the cut core, make two loops out of **Number 6** as shown above from right to left threading it back through them so that it points up the whip. Tighten it and place its end into the loop of the fall. You will need to burns it ends for this.

Ensuring that the whip is securely in the vice, pull the fall down bringing its loop to the top of where you tied the six cords. Once it rests on the first cord tied, pull even harder, this will eliminate any gaps between the cords loops. Cut all 6 cords an inch from the falls loop and the end of the whip end, and burn their ends.

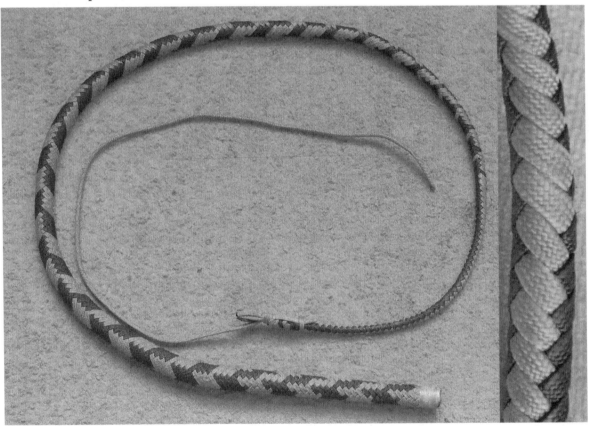

Above shows the whip rolled with the far right photo showing where the gap was on the last drop. Roll this for, as many times as you wish, it will look better.

Roll the end knot once and very lightly or else you may loosen it.

Making the 14 and 12 bight knots

As an introduction to knots for those who are not that familiar with them, I will explain the parts of the pineapple knots I give instruction for in this manual.

Bights – bights are points where the lace bends by 90 degrees and changes direction at the top and bottom of knots, indicated by the black and white arrows in the photo to the left. Bights also determine a knots width.

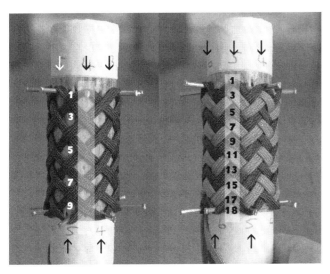

Parts – This is the number of cords, which cross over one another from the top to bottom of the knot as indicated on the left. They dictate the length of a knot.

Foundation Knot – This knot is a Turks-head and is the starting point for a two-cord pineapple knot that I use for all whips.

Interweave knot – This knot is another Turks-head of identical number of parts and bights which is woven into the foundation to create the pineapple knot

So essentially both the knots in this book are two identical Turks head knots woven into one another

The larger of the two knots, which I use on all three types of whips, is based on a 7 bight, 9 part Turks head. Hence why the finished pineapple knot is called a 14 bights and 18 parts pineapple. The good news about this knot is that due to the uneven number of parts for the Turks head, it's called a quick start, meaning that the first initial moves of making it are simple and quick. Into this knot, another Turks knot is woven and this is where the fun starts.

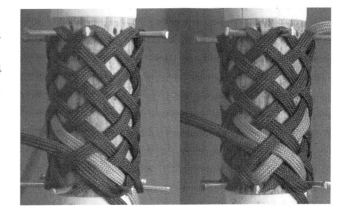

The smaller of the two knots is only used on the Bullwhip for the transition knot. It is based on a 6 bight, 7 part Turks head (which is not a quick knot)

The 14 bight, 18 part Pineapple

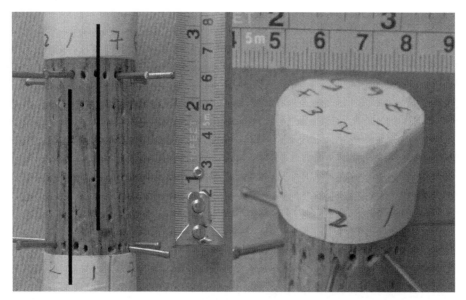

Before starting the knot, you will need to prepare the dowel. Apply masking tape around it at the distance shown above, then use a marker pen to indicate seven points evenly spaced around the dowel. It is safer to mark the nail points this way first before trying to hammer in the nails. Then write the numbers on the masking tape as this will aid in making the knot. Ensure that you mark each corresponding number to the left on the top row.

Remember that the two rows of nails do not run parallel to one another as shown by the black lines.

For simplicity, instead of writing the words **Under** and **Over** for the instructions, I will abbreviate them to **U** and **O** which will hopefully avoid any confusion, plus all instruction will correspond to the photo above them going from left to right.

A typical line of instructions is abbreviated below;

Up…….. 4 to1……. – **O3, U1, O1, U1**

Up - indicates the direction you will thread the cord. In this case from the bottom to the top.

4 to 1 – indicates the nail number you will be braiding from and to. In this case, number 4 on the bottom row to number 1 on the top row going around the dowel in a left to right direction. When it comes to braiding the interweave knot this number will correspond to the middle point between that number and the one proceeding it.

O3, U1, O1, U1 – This is the braiding instruction, if added together, it tells you how many cords you will go across, in this case 6. Starting from nail number 4, you go Over 3 cords, then Under 1, Over 1 and Under the last cord before you get to nail number 1. As the knot progresses, these instructions will become longer. All you need do is keep counting the cords you cross plus as the knot progresses you will see its pattern emerge.

One last thing, the cord will twist as you braid the knot, you need it to lay flat. It is better to un-twist it as you go at this stage as trying to un-twist it on the whip is a nightmare. As the **O** and **U** increase, thread each at a time, and take you time.

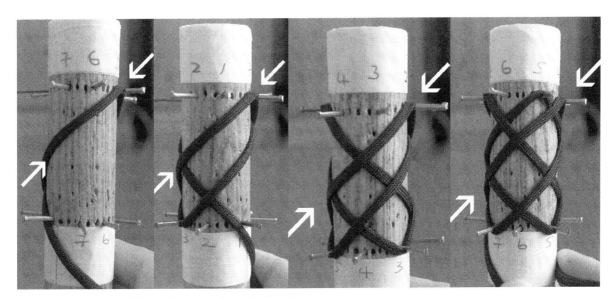

Starting with the 7 bight, 9 parts Foundation knot;

Up 1 to 5 - no U or O. **Down** 5 to 3 - O 1. **Up** 3 to 7 – O1. **Down** 7 to 5 - O2.

Up 5 to 2 - O2. **Down** 2 to 7 - O3. **Up** 7 to 4 - O3. **Down** 4 to 2 - O4, U1.

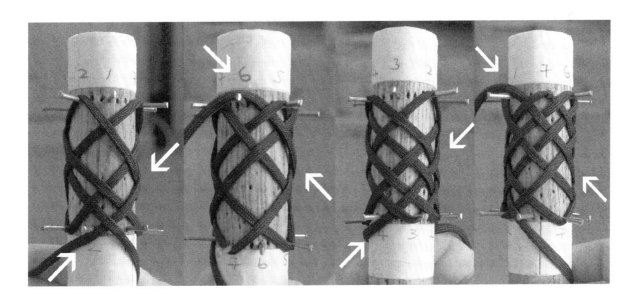

Down 4 to 2 - O4, U1. **Up** 2 to 6 - O4, U 1. **Down** 6 to 4 - O3, U1, O1, U1.

Up 4 to 1 - O3, U1, O1, U1.

Down 1 to 6 - O2, U1, O1, U1, O1, U1. **Up** 6 to 3 – O2, U1, O1, U1, O1, U1.

Down 3 to 1 - O1, U1, O1, U1, O1, U1, O1, U1. To finish go **Up** 1 to 5 O1, U1.

Starting with the 7 bight, 9 part, interweave knot to make the 14 bight, 18 part pineapple knot, Showing the circular movements on a flat photo is difficult so from now on two photos will help to display the full run from top to bottom or vice versa.:

Start by threading the cord between nail numbers 1 and 7 on the bottom row.

Up 1 to 5 - U1, O1, U1, O1, U1, O1, U1, O1, U1.

Down 5 to 3 - U1, O1, U1, O1, U1, O1, U2, O1 U1.

Up 3 to 7 - U1, O1, U1, O1 U1, O1, U2, O1, U1.

Down 7 to 5 - U1, O1, U1, O1, U2, O1, U2, O1, U1.

Up 5 to 2 - U1, O1, U1, O1, U2, O1, U2, O1, U1.

Down 2 to 7 - U1, O1, U2, O1, U2, O1, U2 O1, U1

Up 7 to 4 - U1, O1, U2, O1, U2, O1, U2, O1, U1.

Down 4 to 2 - U2, O1, U2, O1, U2, O1, U2, O2, U1.

Up 2 to 6 – U2, O1, U2, O1, U2, O1, U2, O2, U1.

Down 6 to 4 – U2, O1, U2, O1, U2, O2, U2, O2, U1.

Up 4 to 1 – U2, O1, U2, O1, U2, O2, U2, O2, U1

Down 1 to 6 – U2, O1, U2, O2, U2, O2, U2, O2, U1

Up 6 to 3 – U2, O1, U2, O2, U2, O2, U2, O2, U1

Down 3 to 1 – U2, O2, U2, O2, U2, O2, U2, O2, U1.

To finish **Up** 1 to5 – U2, O2, U2.

Next step is to take the nails off and tighten the knot. Do this gently; you only want to take the excess cord out of the parts of the knot to make it easier to place onto the whip. The photo below shows the knot tightened on the dowel.

This is also a good time to get rid of all those twists in the cord that you could not avoid while braiding it.

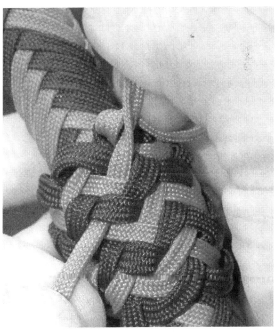

The 12 bight, 14 part Pineapple knot.

To prepare for this knot place 6 nails in two rows using the same size dowel as before and placing the nails the same distance from one another as you did for the larger knot.

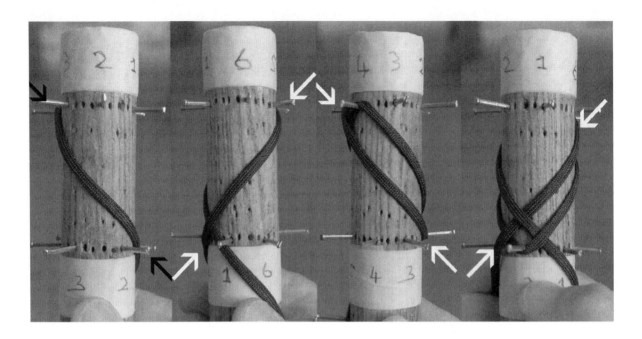

Up 1 to 4 – no O or U. **Down** 4 to 2 – O1. **Up** 2 to 5 – O1. **Down** 5 to 3 – U1, O1.

Up 3 to 6 – U1, O1. **Down** 6 to 4 – O1, U1, O1. **Up** 4 to 1 – O1, U1, O1.

Down 1 to 5 – U1, O1, U1, O1.

Up 5 to 2 – U1, O1, U1, O1. **Down** 2 to 6 – O1, U1, O1, U1, O1.

Up 6 to 3 – O1, U1, O1, U1, O1. **Down** 3 to 1 – U1, O1, U1, O1, U1, O1.

Finish as shown on the first photo below Up 1 to 4 – U1.

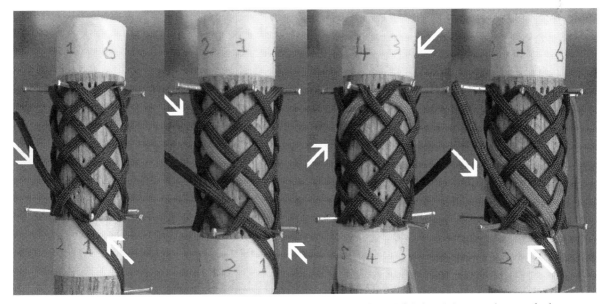

Starting with the 6 bight, 7 part, interweave knot to make the 12 bight, 14 part pineapple knot, Showing the circular movements on a flat photo is difficult so from now on two photos will help to display the full run from top to bottom or vice versa.:

Start by threading the cord between nail numbers 1 and 6 on the bottom row.

Up 1 to 4 – U1, O1, U1, O1, U1, O1, U1.

Down 4 to 2 – U1, O1, U1, O1, U1, O1, U2.

Up 2 to 5 – U1, O1, U1, O1, U1, O1, U2.

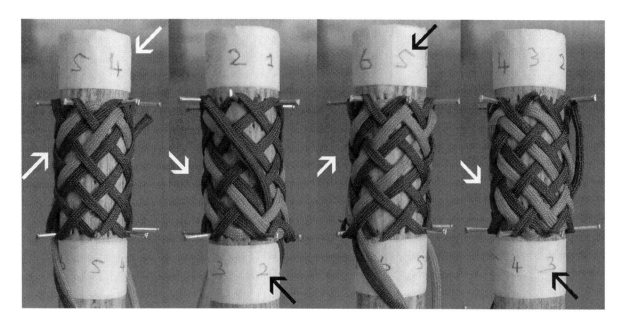

Down 5 to 3 – U1, O1, U1, O1, U1, O2, U2.

Up 3 to 6 – U1, O1, U1, O1, U1, O2, U2.

Down 6 to 4 – U1, O1, U1, O1, U2, O2, U2.

Up 4 to 1 – U1, O1, U1, O1, U2, O2, U2.

Down 1 to 5 – U1, O1, U1, O2, U2, O2, U2.

Up 5 to 2 – U1, O1, U1, O2, U2, O2, U2.

Down 2 to 6 – U1, O1, U2, O2, U2, O2, U2.

Up 6 to 3 – U1, O1, U2, O2, U2, O2, U2.

Down 3 to 1 – U1, O2, U2, O2, U2, O2, U2.

To finish, **Up** 1 to 4 – I1, O2, U2.

Below is the knot tightened up on the dowel.

Knot foundation.

It is only the Bullwhip that has both the top knot (14 bight x 18 parts) and the transition knot (12 bight x 14 parts) placed onto it. The Snake and the wooden handled whip only need the top knot.

To aid placing the foundations of the knot onto the whip, it is best to tie the whip as shown above, by first wrapping the fall around and tying off, securing further with masking tape.

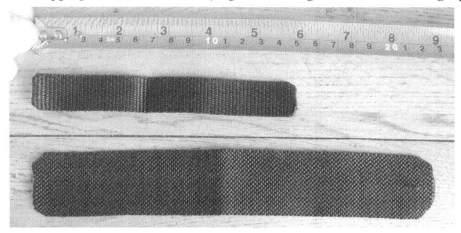

First, cut your webbing to length, 6 inches for the small transition knot and 9 inches for the larger top knot. Burn the ends then snip off the corners and burn again. Snipping the corners stops them from poking out, which does happen as you tightly apply the sinew.

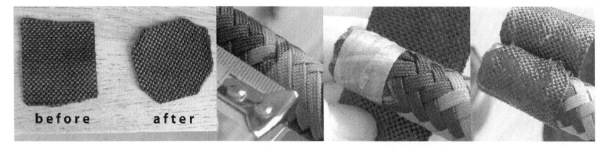

Cut a square piece of webbing that hides the top of the whip workings, burn its edges then snip the corners and burn again. Next you need to mark where to apply the transition knot, to do this find the end of the steel pin, i.e. 7 inches from the top, then make a mark a half of an inch back from the end of the pin.

Next using the widths of both straps, apply glue onto the whip making sure you do not spread it beyond their widths. For the top knot, measure from the very edge of the whip and for the transition knot, try to only apply a fingers width. Once the glue is applied, spread around the whips circumference with your finger.

Also, apply glue to the straps and the top piece, spreading it all over the surface with your finger. Leave the glue to dry for a couple of minutes, and then apply the top strap as shown above. Spread more glue over the side of the strap that does not have any and spread as before.

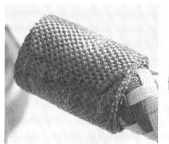   

Once this second layer of glue has dried, place the strap around the whip; the 9 inches should enable the strap to be wrapped around the whip three times.

Cut a 2m length of sinew. Tie a constrictor knot onto the wrapping, pull tight and wind the cord around either side of the knot, tie off and leave the ends hanging.

Apply glue to the end of the whip and down the sides for a fingers width, spread and allow to dry. Next apply the top piece of webbing over the end ensuring you apply it centrally and press the edges down. Wrap the ends of the sinew around the edges of this top piece and tie off. Lastly run the lighter over the coarse edge created by this top piece and smooth it all down.

Apply the wrapping for the transition knot the same as you did for the top knot, ensuring that you place the strap centrally over the mark you made earlier.

You can apply the knots straight onto the foundations now, but it does not hurt to allow the glue in them to dry over night and set stronger.

Attaching Knots.

Use the awl to tighten the knots by first using it to raise up the cord between the Unders and placing your thumb over it to aid pulling as shown in the second photo down.

The best way to attach knots such as these, i.e. two cord knots, is to tighten the inner or last interweave you braided on. On these knots, that was the lighter cord. The reason for this is that they are the inner of the two interweaves; when you tighten the darker interweave it will press down on the lighter interweave, whereas the lighter interweave presses down directly onto the foundation. This is advantageous for two reasons;

1, it enables you to ensure that the knot does cover the foundation – being nylon cord it can tend to stray up and over it.

2, it makes the tightening of the darker knot far easier especially at the parts. This would be the opposite case if you tighten the darker knot first.

The photo above shows from left to right, the top knot positioned over the foundation before the tightening starts, note the distances it rides over the foundation, the knot needs to be above and below the foundation. The last two photos show the lighter interweave tightened. Note how the top and bottom of it cover the foundation, this acts not only to hide the foundation on the bottom but also to anchor it in place.

As you tighten the darker of the interweaves, its helps to keep your thumb over the parts, or the end of the knot as you tighten to stop it riding up over the foundation and the first interweave. The last three photos shows the knot fully tightened onto the foundation. Cut the ends of the cord off as you gently pull them, this ensures that the ends ride up slightly into the knot and hide them. Run the lighter quickly over them to clean up any frayed ends.

Lastly roll the knot on the granite as you did the whip.

Apply the smaller transition knot with the same principles described for the top knot.

Snakewhip

Paracord measurements for 4 foot whip

measurements for other lengths of whip - divide each length below by 4, then times by the length of whip you need. i.e 1st layer , number 3 strand, for a 6 foot whip would be;

1.2 / 4 = 0.3 x 6 = 1.8m.

Core

Lead shot	7	11	17 inches
Paracord core	15	21	30 inches

1st layer

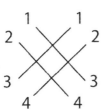

1 = 1m
2 = 1.1m
3 = 1.2m
4 = 1.5m

Sinew to 5 inches

Braid to 2 3/4 ft

2nd layer

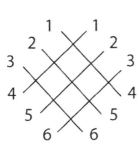

1 = 1m
2 = 1.3m
3 = 1.4m
4 = 1.6m
5 = 1.9m
6 = 2.3m

Sinew to 9 inches

3rd layer

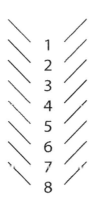

1 = 1.1m
2 = 1.5m
3 = 1.7m
4 = 1.9m
5 = 2.1m
6,7 & 8 = 2.5m

Fall & Knots (these lengths stay the same regardless of whip length)

Fall = 1.5m,
14 bight = 2 x 1.8m
12 bight = 2 x 1.5m

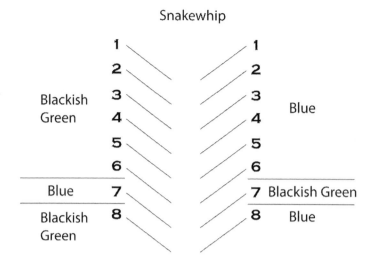

Snakewhip

Illustrated above are the colours I used for this whip and the order I applied them to the 3rd layer.

A Snakewhip is essentially a bullwhip but with a flexible handle. Therefore, the only difference in its construction compared to the bullwhip is the core. You braid the 1st, 2nd and 3rd layer in the same way as the bullwhip, dropping the cords in the same places.

You will note the differences in the lead shot measurements compared to the bullwhip, they are longer to account for the lack of a steel pin.

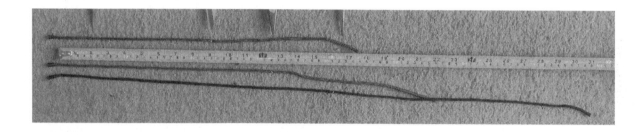

Using the measurements for the lead shot, make the three cords for the core as described for the bullwhip as shown above, ensuring you leave 1 inch of empty cord at the ends this time.

This one inch of cord is glued to a 4-inch piece of steel pin as shown above. The steel pin will only go into the finished whip as far as the top knot, giving the knot a solid base. The other three inches will; be cut off eventually, but aids in the braiding of the layers in providing a solid base to apply into the vice.

Apply the sinew as normal from the ends of the cords on the steel pin and loosely wrap down to the end of the first lead shot returning to the transition of steel pin and lead shot.

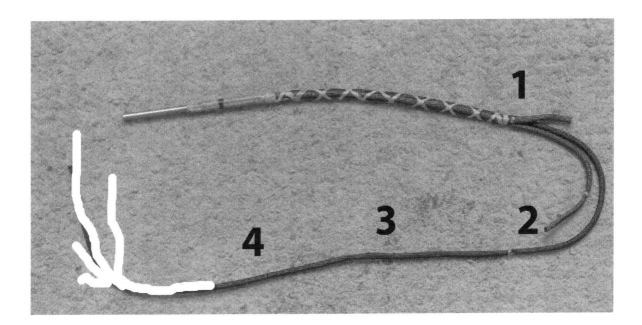

Above shows, the dropping of cords for the 1st layer which is the same as it was with the bullwhip, the white lines indicating end of the 1st layer leaving the four loose cords. Below illustrates the placing of the 1st layers cords on the steel pin in the vice.

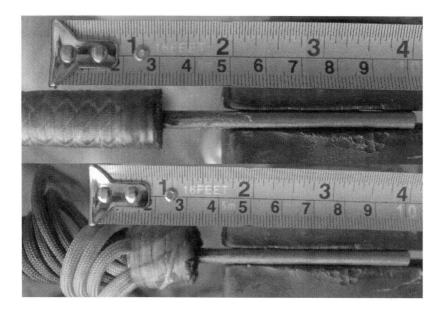

When you attach the cords for the 3rd layer, cut off the excess cords from the 1st and 2nd layers and burn the ends but **do not** cut off the steel pin as you would with a bullwhip, the solid base it provides is still used in the braiding of the 3rd layer. Do not cut if off until you come to apply the top webbing piece for the top knot.

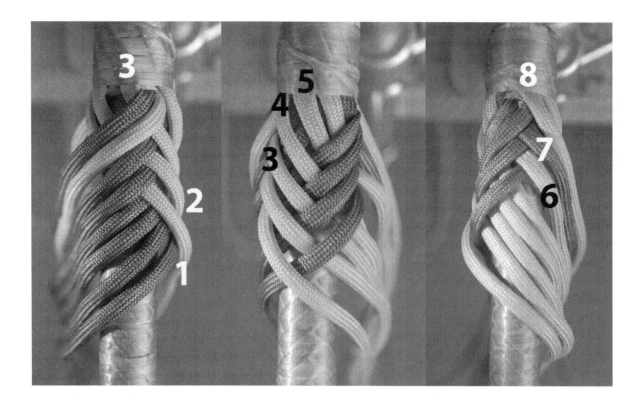

The start braid for the Snakewhip begins with the pair of shorter cords and is the 4 under and 4 over sequence you braided along the whip of the bullwhip. For this reason you set up the cords of the 3rd layer differently as thus;

Again, these instructions in the photos above go from bottom to top for each cord.

Number 1, O4, U4. **Number 2,** U1, O4, U3. **Number 3**, U2, O4, U2. **Number 4,** U3, O4. **Number 5,** U4, O2. **Number 6,** O1, U3. **Number 7,** O2, U2. **Number 8,** U1 if you can.

To carry on this braid, the sequence is as below.

Number 1, under 4, over 4. **Number 2,** under 4, over 4.

Carry on braiding in this sequence until you reach the point at which you start dropping cords as indicated for the bullwhip.

Wooden Handled Whip

Wooden handled whip

Coyote Brown	7 5 2	7 5 2	Coyote Brown
Golden	4 1	4 1	Golden
Blackish Green	3 6 8	3 6 8	Blackish Green

For this whip I used a different way to apply the 3rd layer cords which enable all or most of the colours to run down the whip and not be dropped at intervals, as is the case with the two previous patterns.

As you will note, I have used three colours. You need 300ft for this length of whip so there is no reason why you could not use three colours if you buy 100ft lengths of Paracord. The secret (as such) is to mix up the lengths of cord as illustrated above. Just make sure you have both sets of cords in order when you put them on, this time starting with number 8, number6, number 3 and so on.

Apart from the difference the wooden handled whip is essentially a Snakewhip with a wooden handle, so its construction is the same as the snake, although if you wished you could shorten the amount of lead shot in the shorter of the three core cords by upto 2 inches to make it taper quicker.

The core cords are cut the same length as those of the Snakewhip but leave 3 inches empty at the

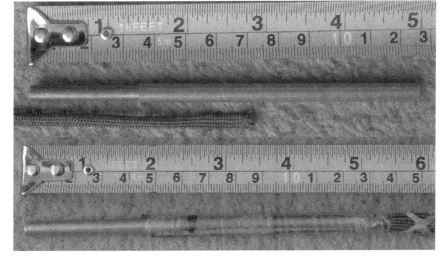

end as shown to the left.

The steel pin for this whip is slightly different in that you will slide it into a shorter piece of copper tubing.

The length of the steel pin is 5 inches and the copper tubing 3 1/2 inches, which with a 6mm outer diameter and a 5mm inner diameter, slides snugly into the steel.

Once you have finished the 2nd layer, mark down 2 1/5 inches from the end of the steel pin/copper tubing and cut away the cord. Burn the end and insert into the wooden handle.

With the steel pin inserted, drill a hole through the wood and steel pin to the other side. I use a 2mm HSS drill bit, then cut one of the lost head nails to 114mm and place into the hole. This ensures that the whip and handle are securely joined together.

The cords of the 3rd layer are attached to the wood and are fixed in place the same way as they are for the bullwhip, the starting and continuous braid is the same as for the Snakewhip i.e. under 4, over 4 sequence.

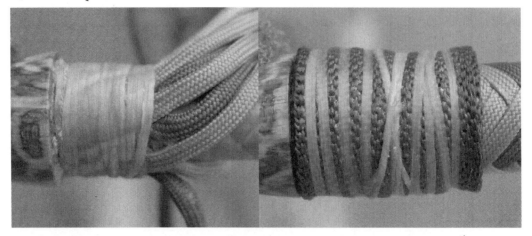

Cover your handle with cloth to protect it whiles you have it in the vice for the 3rd layer braiding. Roll as before when finished and lastly apply the foundation for the knot s as before.

Wooden handle dimensions

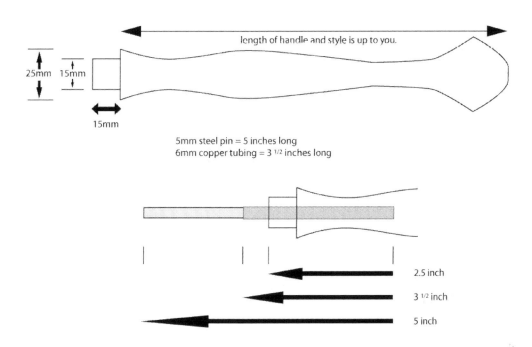

length of handle and style is up to you.

25mm   15mm

15mm

5mm steel pin = 5 inches long
6mm copper tubing = 3 ¹/² inches long

2.5 inch

3 ¹/² inch

5 inch

The one difficulty in making a wooden handles whip is that unless you, or you know someone who has a lathe, you won't be able to make this whip as they are not readily available to buy.

Despite that, I have included the measurements of the one's I make.

I am not an expert in woodturning with my only experience being to make my own whip handles for the last 2 years. If you are just starting out in this hobby/skill, then seeking professional advice/training is best.

The advice I write below is just from my own experiences and not necessarily the best way to do things.

I mostly try to use blocks of wood of 1 ½ x 1 ½ x 12 inches long, called blanks. The woods that I have found most suitable for handles is the dark, dense hard woods such as ebony, Blackwood and snake wood (the one used on this whip), but they tend to be very expensive. Rosewood and cocobolo are good introductory woods that polish to a great finish. You could use the readily available native woods such as Oak, Yew, Elm, but they are quite light in colour and are harder to polish. For a beginner, rosewood is the best.

Most if not all can be obtained from here - http://www.exotichardwoodsukltd.com/

Below is displayed the finished blank with both end blocks of wood

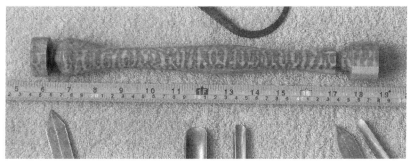

Tools

I have an old Axminster lathe that enables me to turn a blank of upto 13inches long. I use a small band saw to round the blank off and roughing out gouges and a spindle gouge to get the wood down to the shape I need, plus a parting chisel to cut the end the whip goes into and the deep grove for the end of the handle.

Sanding is next and the general rule I use is; starting from roughest to smoothest, for every change in grade I double the sanding time. I use 60 to 120 grade paper for roughing out any nicks or ridges caused by the turning, 180 to 340 removes any marks made by the previous grades and smooth's the blank further. OOO grade wire wool can be helpful but only with the denser woods, do not use on the native woods. Lastly, I rub Lustre and then Vonax onto the blank. These are compounds not paper and I apply them while the blank is turning and rub off with a cotton cloth. Repeat the last two for great results.

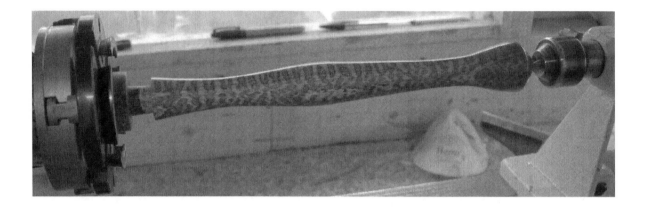

To remove the blank I saw it off at the handle end with a mitre saw while it is still in the lathe, then place the handle in a chuck to sand the handle end. I ensure the block of wood going into the chuck is at least 30mm long so that it protrudes beyond the chuck as shown below so that it can be safely saw it off while on the lathe. This produces a nice central hole at the end of the handle to help gauge were to drill the hole for the steel pin.

I use the other end of the lathe to help ensure that the handle is level before turning the lathe on.

Lastly I use a drill chuck in the lathe with a 6mm wood drill bit to make the 2 ½ inch deep hole into the handle.

Appendix

Making crackers and attaching them to the fall.

I make my crackers from waxed Dacron thread, it is originally made for bowstrings, but I find it is just as good for crackers.

My crackers are 8 ply and upto 8 inches long. First as shown below, I get 4 lengths of 32 inch, then half that. At the half waypoint, I slightly twist the strands and place over the Paracord needle on the vice.

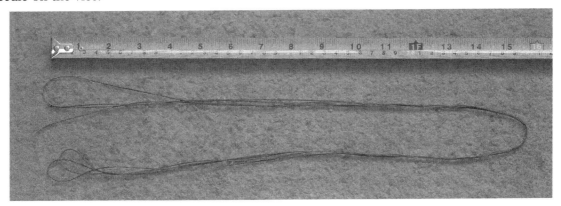

In order to twist two strands together without them unraveling you need to twist each strand in one direction while you place each strand together in the opposite direction as shown below.

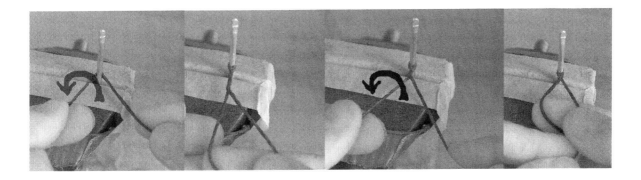

Once you reach the desired length, tie them off as shown below. From left to right – loop over then under, then into the loop once and twice before tightening the knot and then cut about 2 inches beyond the knot.

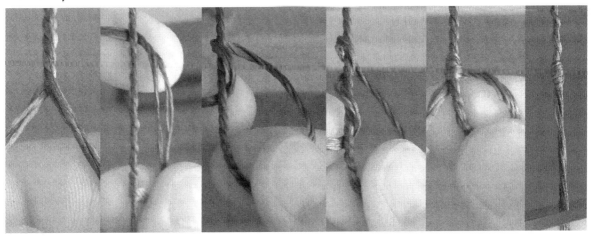

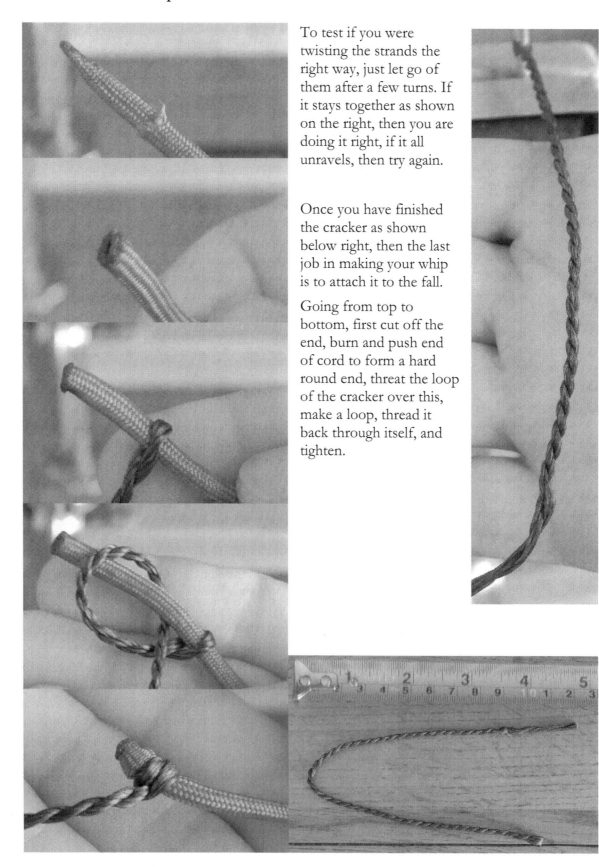

To test if you were twisting the strands the right way, just let go of them after a few turns. If it stays together as shown on the right, then you are doing it right, if it all unravels, then try again.

Once you have finished the cracker as shown below right, then the last job in making your whip is to attach it to the fall.

Going from top to bottom, first cut off the end, burn and push end of cord to form a hard round end, threat the loop of the cracker over this, make a loop, thread it back through itself, and tighten.

Constrictor Knot

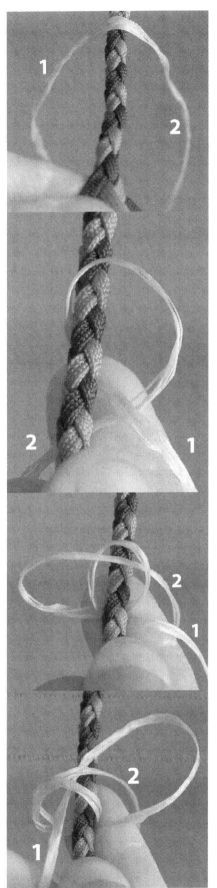

The Constrictor knot is a very useful and simple knot to quickly secure anything together and if I didn't know any different, could have been made for whip making.

Starting on the left photo from top to bottom, and then the right photo from top to bottom –

1, cut a length of sinew (about 1m) and drape over the braid.

2, Fold 1 over 2 and 2 under 1.

3, thread number 2 through the loop leaving it hanging above number 1.

4 Thread number 1 over number 2 and then through the two loops.

5, Tighten knot. When you come to do this for the dropping of cord during the 3rd layer, you will tighten as said but also pull each of the cords your dropping and tighten the sinew again.

6, Cut sinew as near to braid as possible allowing enough for securing.

7, Burn sinew ends and press onto knot.

Cord Breaks

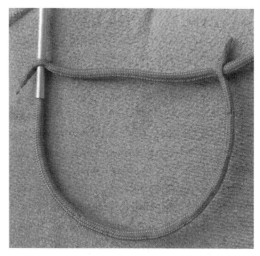

Cord breaks with Paracord are very unusual, in fact the only time I have broken a cord is when I left the lighter too near to a cord while trying to burn the sinew during a dropping of cords. One good reason why you should watch what you are doing while doing the same thing.

The remedy is similar to how I fix broken leather lace, but just like with leather it does leave a bulge along the braid and may affect the whips performance.

But if it happens this fix should mean it's not the end of the world and you will still have a useable whip.

Starting on the left photo from top to bottom, and then the right photo from top to bottom –

1 and 2, melted ends are cut level and treated as for threading into a Paracord needle.

3, make holes near both ends with the awl.

4 and 5, using either the pliers or a needle if you have a long enough piece of cord to do so, thread the short cord from the braid into the hole of the broken

off length.

6, thread a needle onto the end of the longer cord and thread through the short cords hole.

7 and 8, pull the two cords and join together.

8, cut off the ends as close to the fix as possible and burn ends of Paracord and flatten join.

Holding and Pulling cords while braiding..

One of the reason why most people find making a whip difficult, is due to the fact that you must do all the braiding while trying to keep all of the cords tight to an even degree on both sides. It is not easy, but is the only way to get a straight braid as shown along the whip thong on the right.

The photo on the left show the sequence I use for each cord, how I position my hands and use my fingers to try to keep hold of the cords without letting them go. This sequence in actual terms of time takes less than a second but it may help to do it in slow motion first while braiding cord from both side to help create that even amount of force needed for the even pattern in the right photo.

From top to bottom

1, X is the cord I will braid and which I have just pulled tight (as shown below).

2, I have transferred X over to the lower fingers of my right hand keeping it tight between them, releasing my left hand to re-grip the left cords.

3, the right hand cords have been bunched up within my right palm and bottom fingers as I finish the braid and transfer X back to my left hand.

4, The hands and fingers are back to their starting position just before the next cord to be braided is tighten (this cord being top right)

5 and 6 below (5 show front view, 6 a rear view), To tighten the cord to be braided, you will have to let go of all the other cords on that side. Wrap the cord to be tightened under your three bottom fingers and over your index finger, holding it against it with your thumb and

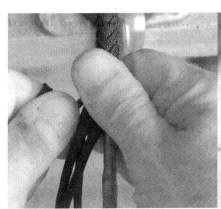

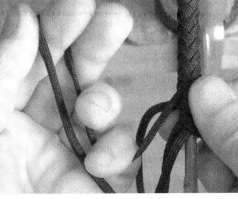

pull sharp and quick while grasping the other side's cords along with the braid to support it.

20123232R00042

Printed in Great Britain
by Amazon